From Start to Finish

MY LIFE AS A MUSLIM

- Trevor Guy
- Sue Mizon
- Paul Morgan

DREF WEN

The Opening

In the name of Allah, Most Compassionate,
Most Merciful.
Praise be to Allah, Lord of the Worlds;
Most Compassionate, Most Merciful;
Master of the Day of Judgment;
You alone we worship, you alone we ask for help.
Show us the straight path,
The path of those whom you have favoured,
Who have not earned your anger nor gone astray.

Special Photography Pat and Charles Aithie (ffotograff)

Design Michael Leaman Design Partnership

The books in this series are also available in Welsh-language editions.

Photographs Philip Jones Griffiths (Magnum) page 12 foot; Trevor Guy (ESIS) pages 12 centre, 14 foot and centre, 28 foot, 30 foot left and right; Mark Hannaford title page centre, pages 4/5 foot, 6 top; Paul Morgan (ESIS) page 12 top; Peter Sanders Library page 6 foot. All other photographs are by Pat and Charles Aithie (ffotograff). Some of these (often indicated by corner mountings) are reproduced from photographs kindly provided by the families concerned. *Map* Julian Baker Illustrations page 7. We have made every effort to contact owners of copyright material and apologise if in any instance we have been unsuccessful.

© Qualifications, Curriculum and Assessment Authority for Wales 1999.
These materials are subject to copyright and may not be reproduced or published without the permission of the copyright owner.
The right of Trevor Guy, Sue Mizon and Paul Morgan to be identified as authors of this book
has been asserted by them in accordance with the Copyright, Designs and Patents Act 1988.
First published 1999 by Gwasg y Dref Wen, 28 Church Road, Whitchurch, Cardiff CF14 2EA. Telephone 029 20617860.
Reprinted 2001.
Printed in Hong Kong.

All rights reserved. No part of this publication may be reproduced or transmitted
in any form or by any means without the prior written permission of the publisher.

Contents

My community 4
How my religion began 6
Starting out in life 8
Following the path 10
What we believe 12
Right and wrong 14
Daily life 16
Growing up 18
Worship at home 20
Worship in the mosque 22
Getting married 24
Fasting and festivals 26
Working for others 28
What happens when we die? 30
Index 32

My community

Amin: I enjoy school. I have lots of friends there and they treat me well.

AMIN My name is Amin Mamown Amin. I'm ten years old and I go to Ninian Park Primary School in Cardiff.

My parents were both born in **the Yemen**. My father, Mamown, came to Wales many years ago. He used to work in a factory but now he has retired. My mother only came to Cardiff later, when she married my father. My sister, Eman, is at university but my younger brother, Almansoor, goes to school with me. My grandfather and grandmother usually live in the Yemen but they are staying with us at the moment.

My family are all **Muslims**. We worship at a **mosque** near the docks in Cardiff. People from many different countries come to our mosque; but most are from the Yemen. We have built a Yemeni Community Centre at the back of the mosque.

Amin: Visiting our relatives in the Yemen is a great adventure. It's very different from Cardiff.

MARWAN My name is Marwan Ghannam. My family live in the village of Menai Bridge on the island of Anglesey in North Wales. I am twelve years old and in my first year at the local comprehensive school. It is called Ysgol David Hughes. My father is a doctor.

It's good being part of a Muslim community because you get to do activities with your Muslim friends as well as with other friends. It also helps you realise you're not on your own.

THINK ABOUT:

Why do you think they have built a Yemeni Community Centre at the back of Amin's mosque?

Marwan says his mosque is a bit of a mess at the moment because of the building work. Do you think the sort of building that is used to worship God matters?

The people at both mosques come from many different countries. Why do most of them come from countries outside the British Isles?

Marwan: The Rukiya Mosque in Damascus is much bigger than ours in Bangor.

Hanadi: Here we all are. Marwan is on the right. Obadah's resting on my knee and Talha's sitting between Mam and Dad.

HANADI

My name is Hanadi. I'm Marwan's sister and I'm fifteen years old. Marwan and I go to the same school. Our younger brothers, Obadah and Talha, are still in primary school.

At school, some of our lessons are in English and some are in Welsh. At home, we speak Arabic because my parents come from Damascus in **Syria**. My mother used to teach Arabic at college.

FACT FILE

The Yemen A hot dry country in the south of the Arabian Peninsula. Most of the people there are Muslim. Many Yemenis came to Cardiff as merchant seamen in the days when it was one of the biggest ports in the world.

Muslims People who follow the religion called Islam. Islam means submission or obedience. Muslims are obedient to God.

Mosque A Muslim place of worship.

Syria Another country where most people are Muslim. It is to be found at the eastern end of the Mediterranean Sea.

Marwan: Our mosque is near the football ground across the Menai Straits in Bangor. It's a bit of a mess at the moment because we are in the middle of building work there.

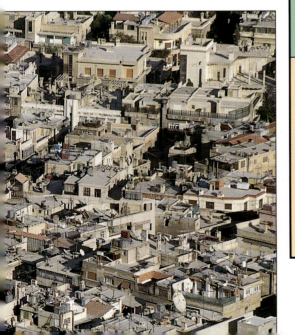

THINGS TO DO

Although Amin and Marwan live in Wales, they have relatives in faraway countries. Do you know where your parents were born or where you have relatives? Compare this with the others in your class. Make a list of the different places from which they come. Try to find them in an atlas. Work out whose relatives live furthest away from them.

Marwan's brothers and sister speak Arabic at home. This makes them different from most of their friends at school. Write about some of the things that make your family special.

Draw two columns on your page. Think of some of the advantages and disadvantages of speaking a language that is different from most of your friends. Write them down in the two columns you have drawn.

Speaking a Different Language	
Advantages	Disadvantages

How my religion began

Amin: These Arabs are just like the people of Arabia when Muhammad was alive.

AMIN My favourite subject at school is history. We have been learning about Celtic times. I love stories about long ago – especially the stories we have in **Qur'an** school at the mosque.

Our religion started with Adam who was the first man in the world. He built a special place to worship **Allah** in **Makkah**. It's called the Ka'aba. Ever since then, there have been people who have worshipped Allah.

Ibrahim is an important person for Muslims. In his day, people were worshipping **idols** and the stars, the moon and the sun. He told them that Allah was the only God. He also rebuilt the Ka'aba in Makkah. It's still there today.

MARWAN The most important person for Muslims is Muhammad. In his day, people had forgotten all about Allah and Ibrahim. The people of Makkah had filled the Ka'aba with idols which they worshipped. They lived very bad lives. They treated poor people and orphans and women like dirt and were always fighting wars.

Muhammad hated all this and was very unhappy. So he used to go out to a cave near the city to think about things. One day, something amazing happened there. An angel called **Jibril** spoke to him. Three times Jibril told him to read something and each time Muhammad said, "But I can't read!" After a while, Muhammad realised that Allah was giving him a message.

Marwan: This is the cave on Mount Hira where Jibril spoke to Muhammad.

THINK ABOUT:

Why is Makkah such a special place for Muslims?

Why do you think Muhammad used to go to the cave outside Makkah?

Why do you think that most people in Makkah were not interested in what Muhammad had to tell them?

The Arabian Peninsula

Marwan: At home we have these two Arabic plaques. The top one says Allah and the bottom says Muhammad.

FACT FILE

The Qur'an The book which contains all the messages that the angel Jibril gave to Muhammad.

Allah The Arabic word for God.

Makkah A city in Saudi Arabia. Muslims pray in the direction of Makkah and try to visit it at least once in their life.

Ibrahim The Arabic name for Abraham.

Idols Statues which some people worship as gods.

Jibril The Arabic for Gabriel, one of the most important of God's angels. Muslims believe that angels are created by God to do his work. Usually they are invisible, except when they appear in human form.

Muhammad memorised what Jibril told him and went to tell his family and friends. Some of them believed but most of them weren't interested. Even so, he kept going back to the cave for more messages. As time went by, he told more and more people what Allah wanted them to know. Most of them just laughed at him but some did begin to listen to what Muhammad had to say. These were the first Muslims.

THINGS TO DO

The Ka'aba can still be seen in Makkah today. Imagine that you are a Muslim who is visiting the city. Design a postcard with a picture of the Ka'aba on one side. On the back, write a message to a friend describing how you feel now that you are in the city. You can see the Ka'aba on the card on page 27 and the calendar on page 28.

Think of something that you feel strongly about. What would you say to convince people that what you believe is important? Write it out as though you were making a speech.

Imagine that Muhammad has just returned from the cave and wants to tell his wife, Khadijah, what has happened. Write down what you think they might have said to each other.

Starting out in life

Hanadi: Here I am with Obadah when he was a little baby …

… and this is Marwan!

HANADI There was great excitement when Obadah and Talha were born. Both times we had a party and lots of friends and family came to see us with presents. Mam took it easy for a week while other people did the cooking and washing.

I remember Dad whispering the **adhan** into Talha's ear, as soon as he was born. Dad did the same to me when I was born but I can't remember it. That doesn't matter. As we grow up, we always know that the first words we ever heard were telling us that there is only one God.

A week after both Talha and Obadah were born, we had an **aqiqah** ceremony. Some people in our mosque shave their babies' hair off for this ceremony. It's the Muslims from Pakistan who normally do that. We didn't. We had sheep **sacrificed** instead.

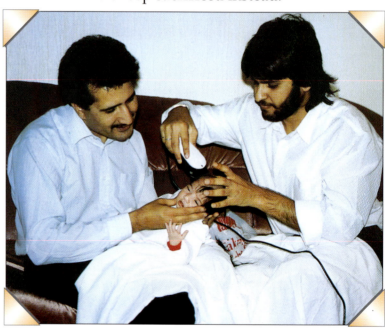

Amin: Adil Mir's parents come from Pakistan. Here his dad is watching him have his hair cut, when he was just a few days old.

AMIN Dad told me that we sent a third of the meat from my aqiqah to relatives. The rest was given to poor Muslims. I was also given my name at that time. I'm proud of being called Amin because it means "honest" or "trustworthy". If I want to be a good Muslim, I have to live up to my name.

THINK ABOUT:

Why do Muslims say the adhan in a new-born baby's ear?

Why do you think Muslims use the meat from the aqiqah sacrifice in the way that they do?

Why did Hanadi's family have parties when her brothers were born?

Amin: You can see Moad and me coming out of the mosque in Cardiff. The other mosque is a famous one in the Yemen.

My best friend, Moad, was born in the Yemen. His name comes from Moad bin Jebel, the man Muhammad sent to take the message of Islam to the Yemen. In Yemeni families, baby boys are **circumcised** when they are eight days old. The Qur'an does not tell us to do that. Muhammad circumcised boys and we follow his example.

FACT FILE

The adhan The Arabic words that are used to call Muslims to come to pray. In English, they are:

Allah is the Greatest!
I bear witness that there is no God but Allah.
I bear witness that Muhammad is Allah's messenger.
Rush to prayer.
Rush to success.
Allah is the Greatest!
There is no God but Allah!

Some of these sentences are said more than once.

Aqiqah The ceremony when children are given their name. Two goats or two sheep are killed if a boy is born; one if it is a girl. The family keeps a third of the meat and gives the rest to relatives and poor people.

To sacrifice To offer something to God. It is a way of saying thank you.

To circumcise To cut off the little bit of skin that covers the end of a boy's penis.

THINGS TO DO

If there were a new baby in your family, what are the first words you would want them to hear? Why would you want to say those words?
Design a colourful card, including your words, that you could give to the baby to keep.

Do you or your friends know of someone who has a new baby in the family?
Can you remember what happened at the time?
How did friends and family feel about it? What did they do?
Act out a short play about it. You could mime it if you wish.

Do you know if your name has a meaning? Does it suit you?
If you have a name book in school, look for a name that you think suits you. If not, make up a name for yourself. You could use a word like Honest which describes what you are like.
Or, you could choose the name of someone who is important to you.
Write a few sentences to say why you have chosen the name.

Following the path

AMIN Every Monday, Tuesday and Wednesday evening, I go to our Yemeni Community Centre with my friend, Moad. We have lessons there about the Qur'an and the things that Muhammad did. Our teacher also teaches us Arabic so that we can read the Qur'an for ourselves.

MARWAN Allah sent lots of **prophets** to the world to tell people how to live properly. Adam was the first prophet. Other important ones were Ibrahim, Yusuf, and Jesus. The last prophet was Muhammad. He could not read or write. Muhammad recited what the angel Jibril told him and his followers wrote it down. The words that they wrote down make up the Qur'an. The different sections in the Qur'an are called **surahs**.

AMIN The Qur'an is very important to us. Some of the surahs make you cry when you hear them read. We wash our hands before we read it to show respect.

Amin: I like Qur'an School because they teach me lots of stories. I like to hear what happened long, long ago: about the prophet's friends and what they got up to in those days.

Marwan: This is some calligraphy from a beautiful mosque in Jerusalem. The words are from the Qur'an.

THINK ABOUT:

Amin says he keeps his Qur'an in a safe place and washes his hands before he reads it. You can see his grandfather using a special stand for the Qur'an in the mosque. Why do you think Muslims take so much care of their holy book?

Why do Amin and Moad spend so much time in Qur'an School?

Why do Muslims memorise parts of the Qur'an?

Amin: Almansoor's rushing again!

There's a shelf in our front room with all sorts of things on it, like photographs, that we want to keep safe. The shelf is just behind my mother's knitting machine. We keep the Qur'an right in the corner.

When I read the Qur'an I don't want to be disturbed because it's so enjoyable. I memorise parts of it so that I can help my brother read it. You should sit down and read a section right through but Almansoor skips over bits. He thinks that doesn't matter; but it does. He says, "I've finished!" Dad says, "Oh no you haven't. You've hardly learnt any of it yet!"

FACT FILE

Prophets People chosen by God to be his messengers and to teach people the right way to live. Muslims believe that Muhammad was the last and greatest prophet that God would send.

Surahs The chapters into which the Qur'an is divided. There are 114 altogether.

Amin: This is Grandad reading the Qur'an.

THINGS TO DO

The Qur'an is sometimes written in beautiful decorative Arabic. This sort of writing is called calligraphy. Copy either the word *Allah* or *Muhammad* to make a colourful calligraphy poster. You can find the words in a picture on page 7.

Some Muslims learn the whole Qur'an off by heart in Arabic. Every good Muslim tries to learn some of it. See if you can learn one of the surahs in English. The first one is one that every Muslim would learn. It is called *The Opening*. You will find it at the front of this book. You could try that one.

If you have a Qur'an in class, you could try one of the short surahs at the end instead.

Muhammad said there had been 124,000 prophets. Only twenty-five are named in the Qur'an. The chart shows those prophets' names in Arabic and English. Try to find out which ones are also found in the Bible. You may know some already. Looking at the index in a Bible will help you with others.

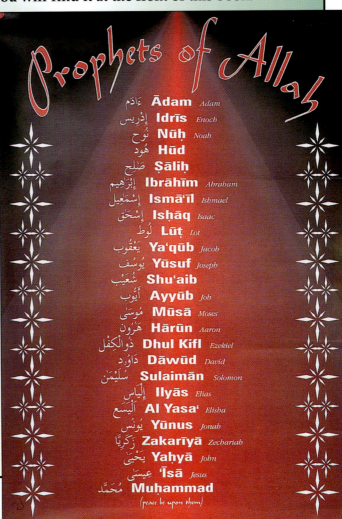

What we believe

AMIN There are five things you must do in Islam. First you have to recite the **shahadah**, which says there's only one God and Muhammad is his prophet. The second is to pray five times a day. The third is to give **zakat**. That means we have to give things to the poor because it's not fair to keep everything to ourselves and become rich. The fourth is fasting in the month of **Ramadan**. The fifth is going on **hajj** to Makkah once in your life if you can afford it.

HANADI We believe that God is one. He is the only one. He is the creator of everything. If you are a Muslim you have to believe these things in your heart and not just say them to fit in. We don't believe that Jesus is God's son.

MARWAN Allah is very kind because he can forgive you lots of things. That shows how kind he is.

Amin: *We call the five things we have to do the Five Pillars of Islam.*

Hanadi: *A lot of people don't believe in God because they say, "There are wars. Why doesn't he stop the wars?" It's not him who starts the wars. It's us.*

THINK ABOUT:

Hanadi mentions one reason why some people don't believe in God. Can you think of any other reasons why people might not believe? Do you believe in God? If you do, what are your reasons?

Amin, Hanadi and Marwan mention a number of things they believe about God. How many can you find?

What does Hanadi mean when she says, "God is one"?

Why do Muslims never draw pictures to show what God is like?

Amin: When we pray, we start by saying, "Allahu Akbar! Allahu Akbar!" That means, "Allah is the Greatest! Allah is the Greatest!"

AMIN We can't imagine what Allah is like. There is nothing like him. When they make films about Islam, they never show God. There's just a light.

Allah has lots of names. On the wall in our house there's a plate with the first surah in the Qur'an on it. It describes Allah. It says he is the Most Merciful and the Most Kind. It also calls him the Lord of the Universe. That means that he is the most powerful person in the whole wide world – in the whole universe.

FACT FILE

The shahadah The first pillar of Islam. Muslims must recite the words, "I bear witness that there is no God but God and Muhammad is the prophet of God."

Zakat A payment to charity. It is another of the five pillars of Islam.

Ramadan The month of the year when Muslims fast during daylight hours. To fast is to go without food and drink. This is another of the five pillars of Islam.

Hajj The pilgrimage to Makkah. A pilgrimage is a journey to a special religious place. Hajj is another of the five pillars of Islam.

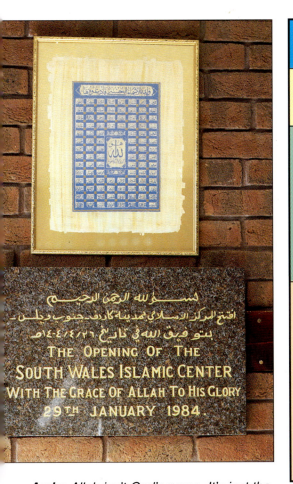

Amin: Allah isn't God's name. It's just the Arabic word for God. His names are written on this poster in our mosque.

THINGS TO DO

Make a list of the five things that all Muslims have to do.

Amin says that Allah has lots of names that describe what he is like. There are ninety-nine different names for God in the Qur'an. *Most Merciful* and *Most Kind* are two of them. Make a note of some names that you think would be good to describe God. Make a poster out of these names. You could work in pairs on this.

Hanadi says that it is no good saying that you believe things just to be able to fit in with the Muslim community. Have you met people who try to make you think they are better than they really are? Sometimes people do this to be respected or to be accepted as part of a group. Make up a short play, or write a story, about somebody who tries to do this but who is shown up for what he or she is in the end.

Right and wrong

AMIN It's not always easy to do what is right. Sometimes, it's like the devil and an angel going around your head. One is saying, "Go on! Do it. Nobody's looking." The other is saying, "Don't do it." Then, there's quite a fight and there's a muddle in your head. It makes you feel all mixed up.

HANADI Muslims are taught to follow **Shariah**. This is a way of life based on what Allah says in the Qur'an and stories about what Muhammad did and said during his life. We call these examples that Muhammad set us the Sunna.

MARWAN Haram and Halal are two important words for Muslims. If something is haram, it is forbidden. Halal means that it is allowed. It is haram to eat animals that eat other animals. That spreads diseases like BSE. **Halal meat** has to be slaughtered by cutting the animal's throat. That is less painful than strangling them. Pork is always haram.

You are not allowed to commit suicide. So I suppose it is wrong to smoke because that shortens your life.

Hanadi: We have lots of books in our mosque to help us understand the right way to live.

THINK ABOUT:

What things help a Muslim decide what is the right or wrong thing to do?

What would a Muslim do if he or she realised that they had done something wrong?

What do you think Amin means when he says, "It's like the devil and an angel going around your head"? Have you ever felt like that?

Amin: This is the special halal butcher's shop where we buy all our meat.

AMIN If somebody tried to persuade me to steal some sweets, I wouldn't do it. I wouldn't want sensible people to see me doing wrong. Even if I were all on my own, there would be one person watching me. That's God.

When I do wrong things, I say, "God, please forgive me. Please give me another chance." Allah lets you off if you do things by accident. If you do it on purpose, that's different. If you do something wrong you can come back to God, but if you keep doing it he won't forgive you.

FACT FILE

Shariah A set of rules or laws about everything that happens in life. The word means a clear, straight path.

Halal meat When animals are killed, Muslims must say *Bismillah Allahu Akbar* (In the name of God, God the Great) for the meat to be halal.

Marwan: What we learn in the mosque helps us in our everyday life.

Marwan: God is always watching over us – even when we're playing football!

THINGS TO DO

At the mosque Amin was told a story about God.

A father had three sons. He gave each of them a sweet and told them to go and eat it where nobody could see them. The youngest went out to the shed and ate his in the dark. The next one went into his bedroom, drew the curtains and locked the door before he ate his sweet. The eldest one just left his in his pocket. When his father asked him why he had done that, he had a simple answer: "There's nowhere where God can't see you!"

Draw some cartoon pictures to retell this story, or think of your own story which makes the same point.

Think of a situation where you might find it difficult to know what is the right thing to do. Write it down and give it to another pupil to decide what he or she would do in that situation. Ask them to give reasons for their answer.

Make a list of things that you think ought to be haram in the classroom. Discuss your list with a partner. Have you written similar things? If you disagree with any that your partner has written, explain why.

Daily life

Hanadi: You could ask anybody at school, "Do you know the girl in the white veil – Hanadi?" They all know me.

MARWAN Some of the people in my class think I'm weird. They are always talking about things I don't do. Even at my age, lots of them boast about drinking alcohol and being drunk. They sneak beer out of the fridge and drink it.

AMIN My friends in school just don't understand some of the things I do because I'm a Muslim. They think I'm a **vegetarian**. When I tell them I'm not, they say, "So, you're having the pork today then?" I can eat chicken or beef or lamb at home but not in school because the meat there isn't halal. That really confuses my friends. They give up and say, "OK. Put your hand up for vegetarian then."

HANADI In most ways, I dress like other girls in my class. I wear normal things like jeans but I don't wear short skirts or shorts or low-cut tops. The only real difference between me and other girls is my scarf. That is like a protection. When you're out, boys see you and know you're a Muslim. So they don't try to chat you up. Some people poke fun at me because of it but my friends understand. They're really good about it.

MARWAN It's prayer that makes our lives so different. Every day, we pray five times. The early afternoon prayer is difficult when we are in school. There's nowhere for us to pray, then.

THINK ABOUT:

Look at the chapter on *Right and wrong*. Why doesn't Amin eat pork?

What sorts of things make Muslims different in their everyday life from non-Muslims?

Why do you think Hanadi dresses in the way that she does?

Hanadi: My friends are older and they are always going on about drinking, boys and smoking. Sometimes, it feels odd that they are going on about it but I'm not.

FACT FILE

Vegetarians People who refuse to eat meat.

Marwan: Here I am, leading the young people in the prayers after Sunday School.

THINGS TO DO

Cut pictures from magazines or brochures to make a scrap book or display showing different ways that people dress. Find one of a Muslim if you can. Write a sentence with each picture saying why you think the person or persons are dressed in the way that they are.

Make a list of five things you do (or try to do) every day because they are good and five things you don't do (or try not to do) every day because they are bad. Talk about the reasons for your lists with a partner.

Are there some things that you would not wear? Are there things your parents do not let you wear? Draw a chart like the one below.

	What they are	Reasons
Things that I would not wear		
Things my parents do not let me wear		

17

Growing up

Marwan: Apart from photographs like Dad's, I've only seen pictures of Makkah on the television. When you go to Makkah, it must be brilliant to see how many Muslims there are in the world.

AMIN We don't have any special ceremonies to show that you have become a Muslim. All you have to do is to say and believe that Allah is the only God and that Muhammad is his prophet. Although I'm only ten and Almansoor is eight, we still have to follow what Allah has revealed to us in the Qur'an.

We don't have to fast in Ramadan until we are twelve but we like to practise. This year, I only missed eight days of fasting out of thirty. I missed those days because I was doing some special activities in school.

MARWAN Muslims have to go on pilgrimage to Makkah. Dad took that photograph on the wall when he went there. I will go one day, too. **Inshallah**. We can't afford to go this year because we are buying a new house. In any case, it doesn't count as hajj until you are about fifteen years old.

THINK ABOUT:

What do you have to do to be a Muslim?

Why did Marwan say "Inshallah" after he said he would go to Makkah one day?

What things will Marwan and Amin be expected to do when they are grown up? Are there things that you will be expected to do when you are older?

Marwan: Brother Jamil has taken over the class that Dad used to teach.

Marwan: Obadah and Talha have fun in their Arabic class, too.

In Qur'an school, Brother Ahmad explains things like zakat or who the prophets are to Obadah and Talha. Hanadi and I used to have lessons like that, when we were younger. But now we are older, we study the Qur'an. Today, we were going through surahs to understand their meaning. This helps us to be able to read the Qur'an for ourselves.

AMIN I like going to Qur'an school because when I grow up I want to be an **imam**. The things I learn there are very important. I have won prizes in quizzes about Islam. We try to learn a lot of the Qur'an off by heart. If I can learn it all, I will be called a hafiz.

FACT FILE

Inshallah The Arabic for "If God is willing".

Imam A Muslim who is respected as a leader or a teacher.

Amin: Sheikh Said is our imam. He knows ever so much and everybody respects him.

THINGS TO DO

Design a certificate or a trophy that could be given to the winner of a quiz on Islam or the Qur'an.

Make a list of things you are not allowed to do now but that you will be able to do when you are older. Make another list of things you do now that you will not do when you are older. Think of reasons why you have to wait until you are older before you do some things.

What do you want to be when you grow up? Try to work out what sorts of things you will have to be able to do for that job. What sort of person will you need to be? Write out a poster advertising the job you would like and describing the sort of person that is needed.

Worship at home

MARWAN I pray five times every day. It's a very important part of my life. Our first prayer is before sunrise. In the summer, that is very early. So we go back to bed after it. Then, there is one early in the afternoon. The next two normally come close together. One has to be done before sunset and the other in the twenty minutes after sunset before it becomes dark. The last one is between then and midnight.

Amin: My friends like going out to play. So do I, but I have to respect my God and pray to him.

THINK ABOUT:

Why is prayer so important to a Muslim?

How is du'a prayer different from doing a rakat?

What does Amin mean when he says that he prays to God with his body as well as with words?

Amin: We pray to God with our bodies as well as with words. When we pray, we do rakats. We say special words and kneel and bend down.

HANADI

Women don't normally go to the mosque to pray. Men and women don't like mixing much and the mosque is crowded with men. So women usually pray at home. We do sometimes go to the mosque to pray but it's a bit far. Even my brothers and my dad pray at home most of the time.

After we've done our **rakats**, we sometimes say **du'a prayers** to ask God to help us. It's a bit like **meditation** because it's so relaxing. You sit there and really concentrate. You concentrate on one thing and look at in different ways. You ask for forgiveness and pray about personal things. Some people recite surahs from the Qur'an. If you don't know any, you can make up your own prayers or just say "Allah" over and over again.

MARWAN

I ask God to let me do well in tests and exams. We're moving because of Dad's job. So I asked for help with the money to buy a new house.

FACT FILE

Rakat A set of movements and words which have to be completed when Muslims pray. Normally, they have to do either two, three or four sets, depending on which prayer time it is.

Du'a prayers Worshippers make these up for themselves after they have done their rakats in Arabic. Du'a can be in the worshipper's own language instead of Arabic.

Meditation Staying still and quiet and thinking about things.

THINGS TO DO

Muslims do their prayers on special mats. Look at the one on this page. It has an arch on it. This reminds Amin of the arch in the mosque which shows the direction of Makkah. Design your own prayer mat. You could use batik or paint a white piece of cloth.

When Marwan and Hanadi say du'a prayers, they pray about what is most important to them at that moment. Write down what you would pray about at the moment, if you had to make up your own prayer. You might like to write this in the form of a prayer.

Hanadi talks about sitting and concentrating on one thing and looking at it in different ways. Try sitting very still for three minutes. Think hard about one thing. Then write down what you thought about. Did anything come to your mind that you had not thought about before? Discuss with others in the class how you felt while you were thinking like that.

Worship in the mosque

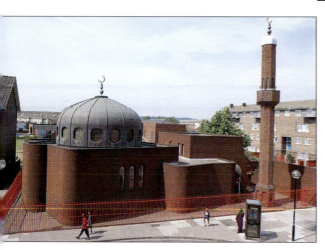

Amin: This is our mosque in Butetown in Cardiff.

AMIN We can pray anywhere but Muhammad said it's best to pray in the mosque. You meet other Muslims, if you do that. God's angels keep a record of everything you do. You score nought if you don't pray at all. If you worship at home, you might have five points; but for praying at the mosque it would be ten.

I like our mosque. It is quite simple but it is decorated with beautiful stained-glass windows and special Arabic writing. At the front, there is an arch in the wall. We pray facing the arch because it shows us the direction of Makkah.

By the arch, there is a pulpit. Sheikh Ibrahim stands in it, when he teaches us on a Friday.

There are two main rooms; one for the women and one for the men. There is a partition that can be opened up to turn the two rooms into one. There are also separate **wudu** rooms for men and women.

We have to be clean to pray, so before we pray we do wudu. We wash our hands, mouth, nose and our whole face. Then, it's our arms up to the elbow. After that, we wipe our damp hands over our hair, our ears and the back of our neck. The final thing is to wash our feet.

We have special prayers at midday on Friday. All the men try to go to the mosque for these. I can only go during school holidays. During the half-term holiday, I went with Almansoor, Dad and Grandad. Before we did our rakats together, Sheikh Ibrahim gave a talk explaining things that the Qur'an teaches.

THINK ABOUT:

What are the main things you would expect to find in a mosque?

Why do Muslims pray in the direction of Makkah?

Why does the imam give a talk at midday prayers on a Friday?

Amin: These are the stained-glass windows in our mosque.

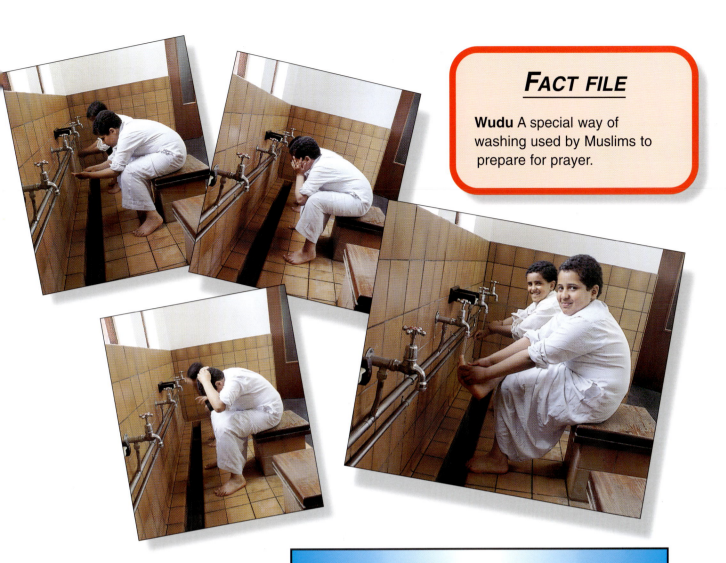

FACT FILE

Wudu A special way of washing used by Muslims to prepare for prayer.

Amin: *Sheikh Ibrahim spoke in Arabic first and then in English.*

THINGS TO DO

At the front of the mosque is a set of clocks showing the times of prayer for the day. Make your own set. Make sure the hands are movable so that they can be changed each day. Work out what time you think prayers would have been today. Show the times on your clocks.

When Amin went to Friday prayers, Sheikh Ibrahim spoke about bringing up children. He said it is better for boys to be honest, trustworthy and brave than to be rich or important. Also, girls should be encouraged to be modest and not to mix with men more than is necessary. Imagine that you have to give the talk. Write out what you would say.

You are going to visit a mosque where you will meet the imam. Prepare for your visit by deciding on the questions you will need to ask to be able to understand what happens when Muslims worship there. Compare your questions with those of the rest of the class.

Getting married

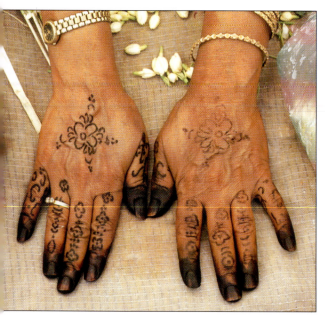

Hanadi: Brides decorate their hands with special patterns as well as wearing special clothes and jewellery.

HANADI Our families usually help us decide who we are going to marry. My Uncle Erfan lives in Syria. His sister, Aunt Ulla, told him that she knew a very nice girl called Mona. She was a great person and would make a good wife. Aunt Ulla showed Uncle Erfan some photographs of her friend and he said he would like to meet her. So the three of them went out for coffee together. Later, he went to Mona's home for a meal with the family. He really did like her. Two years ago, we all went to Damascus for their engagement party. Then, this summer, we went again for their wedding.

Our weddings are more like parties. There is loud music and dancing. It's usually men on their own and women on their own. That way, they have more freedom to do what they want. We don't have a proper meal. We eat special sweets.

Amin: You could hardly hear Sheikh Said even with his microphone.

THINK ABOUT:

What is meant by an arranged marriage? Was Uncle Erfan's marriage arranged?

Why do you think that Muslims sign a contract when their children are married?

Do you think a wedding should a be a religious ceremony?

Amin: The wedding party was really noisy.

FACT FILE

Contract A written agreement. For Muslim weddings, the contract includes a payment that the husband must make to his wife. This is called a dowry.

AMIN I went to a Pakistani wedding with my family in the Cardiff Bay Visitors' Centre. Sheikh Said took the ceremony. It was very simple. The couple were asked if they agreed to marry each other. Then the families signed a **contract**.

It was more like a party than a religious ceremony. It was so noisy that a lady had to stand up and say, "Be quiet. We can't hear at the back." I didn't like the food. It was too hot and spicy.

The bridegroom wore a smart suit. The bride didn't wear white. She wore a beautiful coloured dress and lots of jewellery.

THINGS TO DO

Look at the picture of the bride's hands. Draw a hand showing how you would decorate it for a wedding.

Some Muslim families sign a contract when their children are married. Imagine that you have a son or daughter who is about to be married. What conditions would you want to see in the contract? Write out the contract that you would want.

Write a description of the sort of person that you would like to marry, when you are older.

Amin: This is one of the contracts that Sheikh Said keeps in his office. Can you see what the dowry was that the man paid his wife?

Fasting and festivals

MARWAN In the month of Ramadan, we don't eat or drink between sunrise and sunset. Ramadan is very good but I don't like it at five o'clock in the morning when I have to wake up for breakfast. I like breaking the fast every evening because you wait and wait; then, finally, it's time. It makes you realise the worth of food. The rest of the year it's just food. In Ramadan, you think, "Wow! It's food!"

AMIN Ramadan is the month when Jibril first gave the Qur'an to Muhammad. So there are lots of readings from the Qur'an at the mosque. During the last ten days, some people spend nearly all their time there. Free dinners are served in the evening for anybody who comes.

At the end of Ramadan, we celebrate **Eid ul-Fitr**. Everybody goes out the night before to watch for the new moon. That is the sign that it is time for Eid ul-Fitr to start. Then, in the morning, we all go to the mosque before breakfast.

Eid ul-Fitr is a big family day. We all come together for a special meal. Apart from that, we spend the day visiting and phoning relatives and friends. Lots of people come to see us, too.

THINK ABOUT:

What is special about the month of Ramadan for Muslims?

How do Muslims celebrate Eid ul-Fitr?

Why do Muslims sacrifice at Eid ul-Adha?

Amin: I was so tired for Eid ul-Fitr this year because I'd stayed up watching television.

MARWAN We have our presents on the morning of Eid. So the best part is the night before. I go to bed thinking, "What am I going to get? I hope it's good."

HANADI We put decorations up the night before. We have tinsel and lights so that my little brothers don't feel left out because we don't celebrate Christmas. The visiting goes on for about three or four days. I love mixing with people and eating lots of sweets.

AMIN The other important festival is **Eid ul-Adha**. This is the time when Muslims go on hajj. We remember the story of Ibrahim at this time. Even if we don't go on hajj, we sacrifice animals and give the meat to our neighbours, relatives and poor people.

FACT FILE

Eid ul-Fitr The first of the two main Muslim celebrations. The name means the Festival of Breaking. It celebrates the end, or breaking, of the fasting during Ramadan.

Eid ul-Adha The second main Muslim festival. The name means the Festival of Sacrifice. It takes place on the day when pilgrims on hajj make a sacrifice. They do this to remember how God tested Ibrahim by asking him to sacrifice his son, Ismail. In the end, God gave Ibrahim a ram to sacrifice instead.

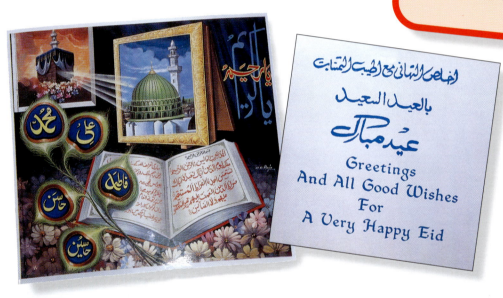

Amin: My friend Hassan, in school, gave me a card during Ramadan. So I gave him one for Eid ul-Fitr.

THINGS TO DO

Make a card that Amin could have given to his friend Hassan for Eid ul-Fitr. You could look through other chapters for ideas for your design. Eid cards often have the words *Eid Mubarak* on them. That means *Happy Eid*.

To get an idea of what it is like for Muslims to fast, try going without breakfast before school for one day. Don't eat until lunch time. Before going to lunch, write down a sentence or two to describe how you feel. Then, after lunch, write another sentence or two to describe how you feel after eating. Check with your parents first, in case there is a health reason why you should not go without food for so long.

Write a note explaining why Marwan says, "Wow! It's food!" during Ramadan. Look at the Fact file on page 13. It will give you the information you need. You could use Marwan's words as a heading.

Working for others

Amin: Families' Relief is another Muslim charity.

MARWAN In our mosque, there is a poster with a **hadith** which says, "**Charity** doesn't make your wealth any less." Allah will always look after you if you give to charity.

AMIN In school, I organised quiz sheets and a Guess the Baby Teacher competition to raise money for Bosnia. We sent the money to **Oxfam**.

We give our zakat at Eid ul-Fitr. Around that time, the postman brings letters from **Muslim Aid** asking us to help Muslims who are in trouble.

They collect zakat in the mosque during the special prayers at the end of Ramadan. The money goes to buy things that refugees need. There aren't a lot of really poor people in our community. So we use the zakat for people abroad.

MARWAN For zakat at Eid ul-Adha, we either slaughter a sheep and give the meat away or we give money. This year, we sent money to Syria. My parents' family slaughtered a sheep for us and gave it to poor people in Damascus.

Amin: There's a box in the mosque where we can put zakat.

THINK ABOUT:

Why doesn't charity make your wealth any the less?

Why do you think that Marwan's family sent its zakat to Damascus?

For what sorts of things do Muslims use zakat?

Amin: There are people with problems all over the world.

HANADI Some people say God must be really cruel or stingy because so many people starve in the world. Well, we're the selfish ones because everybody should be equal. For Zakat you're supposed to give 2.5% of what you've got in the bank. If everybody gave that, it would make a big difference. It would help the world a lot more than just having Red Nose Day.

Things to do

Marwan can remember when his mosque gave a lot of money to other Muslims to build a mosque. Then the community in Bangor wanted to build an extension onto its own mosque. At the last minute, the other Muslims sent the money back. So the extension was built and, in the end, they even had money left over. Write a story in which things turn out all right even though somebody gives a lot away.

How much money do you have at the moment, including your savings? How much zakat ul-Fitr would you have to pay on it? Add up how much the whole class would have to pay, if you all had the same. Decide what you would be able to do to help other people, with this amount of money.

Write a letter to Muslim Aid or Oxfam or any other organisation that helps people in need. Explain why you are writing and ask for information about the work they do. They may be able to send somebody to school to tell you about their work.

Fact File

Hadith Stories about things that Muhammad did or said. Muslims believe these show them the right way to live.

Charity means love or kindness. People often give money or do work to show their charity. Groups that help people in need are called charities.

Oxfam A well-known charity that works with poor people all over the world to improve their lives.

Muslim Aid A charity that helps Muslims in need in many different countries.

What happens when we die?

Hanadi: My grandmother is second from the right in this photograph. We all have to die; but knowing that doesn't stop you being upset when somebody close to you dies.

MARWAN My grandmother died just before Obadah was born. She had a heart attack in Syria. Mam realised that something was wrong but Dad didn't tell her because she was pregnant. He didn't want to upset her. When he told her, I remember Mam crying and lots of people coming to visit her.

HANADI When a Muslim dies, the body is washed and perfumed at the mosque. Then it is covered with white sheets. We say prayers at the mosque before the body is buried at the cemetery. We never **cremate** bodies.

AMIN When you die, you are put into a grave. Then, one day, you will come back to life and will have to speak to Allah.

All through your life, you have an angel on each shoulder. They write down all the good and bad things you do. God will give the angels scales and they will weigh all the things you have done. If most of what you've done is good you'll go to heaven. If it's bad, you'll go to hell. If you argue, the angels will show you what they have written, to remind you.

> **THINK ABOUT:**
>
> Why do Muslims think that Heaven is an amazing place?
>
> How does Allah decide who will go to heaven?
>
> Why do you think Muslims never cremate bodies?

MARWAN Heaven must be an amazing place. It's as if you have a different body when you're there. It's a million times better than this world. Put all the rewards you ever get on the earth together and they're like the smallest one in heaven. Whatever you wish for there will come true. The grapes are ten times sweeter and better in heaven and there's sweet wine there that doesn't make you drunk.

There are different levels in heaven. If you are really good in this world, you will see Allah in Heaven. I think that's where Muhammad will be – in the best place.

Marwan: Heaven must be an amazing place.

FACT FILE

Cremate To burn a body instead of burying it in the ground.

THINGS TO DO

Marwan believes that heaven is a place where you will have everything you wish. Try to picture in your mind your own perfect place. Write a description of what it would be like. Or try to paint a picture of it. You may decide to show your feelings about the place by using shapes and colours that only you can explain. For example, you might use blue because it reminds you of the sea on a happy holiday you have had.

On a plain piece of paper, write down all the words that come into your mind when you think about somebody dying. Are there any happy words on your paper? Which ones are they? Use dark colours to show the sad words and bright colours to show the happy words. You can either go over the letters with colours or shade around each word. Write a sentence to explain why it is possible to write happy words.

If you were Marwan's dad, would you have told your wife about her mother's death? Draw two columns and use them to write down some reasons why you would have told her and some why you would not.

Marwan's Grandmother

| *I should tell my wife now that her mother has died because:* | *I should wait until the baby is born before I tell my wife that her mother has died because:* |

Index

*Page numbers in **black** show Fact file entries.*

Adam 6, 10, 11
adhan 8, **9**
alcohol 16, 31
Allah (*see also* God) 6, **7**, 9, 10, 12, 13, 14, 15, 18, 21, 28, 30, 31
"Allahu Akbar" 13, 15
angels (*see also* Jibril) 6, 7, 10, 14, 22, 30
aqiqah 8, **9**
Arabia 6
Arabian Peninsula 5, 7
Arabic language 5, 7, 10, 11, 13, 18, 19, 21, 22, 23
Arabs 6

babies, shaving head of 8
Bangor 4, 5, 29
Bible 11
boys 23
burial 30

calligraphy 10, 11, 22
Cardiff 4, 5, 9, 22, 25
cards 27
cave of Muhammad 6, 7
charity (*see also* zakat) 13, 28, **29**
Christmas 27
circumcise **9**
clocks 23
clothes (*see also* veil) 16, 17, 24, 25
cremate 30, **31**

Damascus 4, 5, 7, 24, 28
dowry 25
du'a prayer 20, **21**

Eid ul-Adha 26, **27**, 28
Eid ul-Fitr 26, **27**, 28, 29
English language 5, 23

Families' Relief 28
family 4, 5, 8, 26
fasting (*see also* Ramadan) 12, 13, 18, 26, 27
Five Pillars of Islam 12, 13
food 16, 24, 25, 26, 27, 31
forgiving 15
Friday prayers 22, 23

girls 23
God (*see also* Allah) 12, 13, 15, 20, 22

hadith 28, **29**
hafiz (*see also* Qur'an, memorising) 19
hajj 12, **13**, 18, 27
halal 14, 15
halal butcher 14
halal meat 14, **15**, 16
haram 14, 15
heaven 30, 31
hell 30

Ibrahim 6, **7**, 10, 11, 27
idols 6, **7**
imam 19, 22, 23
"Inshallah" 18, **19**
Ismail 11, 27

Jerusalem 10
Jesus 10, 11, 12
Jibril 6, **7**, 10, 26

Ka'aba 6, 7
Khadijah 7

languages (*see also* Arabic, English, Welsh languages) 4, 5, 21, 23

Madinah 7
Makkah 6, **7**, 12, 13, 18, 21, 22
marriage contract 24, **25**
meditation **21**
Moad bin Jebel 9
mosque 4, **5**, 6, 9, 10, 13, 14, 15, 21, 22, 23, 26, 28, 29, 30
Mount Hira 6
Muhammad 6, 7, 9, 10, 11, 12, 13, 14, 18, 22, 26, 29, 31
Muslims 4, **5**, 7, 8, 9
Muslim Aid 28, **29**

names 8, 9
names of Allah 13
new moon 26

Opening, The 2, 11
Oxfam 28, **29**

Pakistan 8, 25
patterns (on bride's hands) 24, 25
pilgrimage (*see also* hajj) 13, 18
poor, the 8, 12, 28, 29
pork 14, 16
prayer (*see also* du'a prayer, rakats) 7, 12, 13, 16, 17, 20, 21, 22, 23, 30
prayer mat 21
prophets (*see also* Adam, Ibrahim, Ismail, Jesus, Muhammad, Yusuf) 10, **11**, 13, 18, 19

Qur'an 6, **7**, 9, 10, 11, 13, 14, 18, 19, 21, 22, 26
Qur'an, memorising (*see also* hafiz) 10, 11, 19
Qur'an school 6, 10, 18, 19

rakats 20, **21**
Ramadan 12, **13**, 18, 26, 27, 28
Rukiya Mosque 4

sacrifice 8, **9**, 27, 28
Saudi Arabia 7
school 4, 5, 6, 16, 18, 28
shahadah 12, **13**
Shariah 14, **15**
Sheikh Ibrahim 22, 23
Sheikh Said 19, 24, 25
smoking 14, 16
stained glass windows 22
stealing 15
suicide 14
Sunna 14
surahs 10, **11**, 13, 19, 21
Syria **5**, 7, 24, 28, 30

vegetarian 16, **17**
veil 16

washing (*see also* wudu) 10, 22, 23, 30
Welsh language 5
women 6, 21, 22, 24
wudu 22, **23**

Yemen, the 4, **5**, 7, 9
Yemeni Community Centre 4, 10
Yemenis 4, 5, 9
Yusuf 10, 11

zakat 12, **13**, 19, 28, 29